Spikenard

Spikenard

Zinnia Hansen

The Seattle Youth Poet Laureate is a special program of
Seattle Arts & Lectures in partnership with Urban Word.

ISBN 9781949166064

Published by Poetry NW Editions
2000 Tower Street
Everett, WA 98201

Distributed by Ingram

PRINTED IN THE UNITED STATES OF AMERICA

Contents

[Untitled] 1

Through the Rain 11

American Poetry 12

Quilting 13

Apart 14

3AM in the City Allen Ginsberg and the Body 15

Revolution 16

Spring 17

Green 19

RED 20

Hunger 21

Free 22

I Don't Know How to Pray 23

Bed Sheets 24

(Metaphorically) 25

Samhain 26

Winter 27

Topless 28

Perfect Forms 29

Between 30

The West 31

From the Shell 32

Rosemary 33

The Heart 34

Panentheism 35

Jump 37

The Earth and the Sun 38

A Place of Worship (Manifesto) 39

The Kitchen 41

Rosewind...43

Saeta 44

Building with Pebbles..45

Iconography 46

The Airport 47

Down the Road.. 48

[Untitled] 50

Orthodoxy 60

Open 61

Mint When It's Raining 63

New Day 64

The Apple 65

Black Velvet... 66

Two Dimensional/Ten Dimensional 67

Respite.. 68

Highways...69

Bathroom Floor 70

I Contain..71

Prayer 72

When the Hermès Ad on the Back
    of Vogue Magazine Spoke to Sappho 73

Capitol Hill Autonomous Zone 74

The Womb 76

Apocalypse, Αποκάλυψις! 77

Imagining 79

Soaked and Screeching 80

Something to Hold Flowers 81

Yellow 82

Spring Salmon in the Skagit Valley 83

My Mama/My Maria 85

Night Kayaking 87

Notes 89

Acknowledgments 91

About the Author 93

Spikenard

I'm going to plant
a garden inside
myself and never
show it to you.

he sticks his shovel into the half-
frozen ground and doesn't
bother to pull it back out. the world
wavers, lamps becoming suns.

this planet is a pomegranate
seed bleeding. I'll need a bone-
saw when the juice is gone.

I'm throwing spears
into the sea,
each a swallowed
opening, like
the hole a worm
digs in the earth.

I'm going to plant
a garden inside
myself and never
show it to you.

                                       he sticks his shovel into the half-
                                     frozen ground and doesn't
                          bother to pull it back out. the world
                                wavers, lamps becoming suns.

this planet is a pomegranate
seed bleeding. I'll need a bone-
saw when the juice is gone.

                                         I'm throwing spears
                                            into the sea,
                                     each a swallowed
                                        opening, like
                                   the hole a worm
                                    digs in the earth.

the moon lives down the lane.
I knock on her door when I want
to be seen with kind eyes
that have watched me become
from a neighbor's distance.

every time I look up
from my book the snow
changes texture.

a tree has blood,
thick blood that fills
its cold fractals
with slow warmth.

drink your wine.
I want to see your face,
flushed and free,
because I've forgotten
how to love red.

Zinnia Hansen

I took a hammer
to my words,
but forgot the nails.
I broke open
the blue sky,
I broke open blue.

God is something
that demands a temple,
a body It's too big for.

the same thing enclosed
in the moon is trapped inside
watermelons and fists.

I want to think
every beautiful
thought at once.

Spikenard

I looked straight
at the sun
and it reminded me
of how I caught
a glimpse
of your breasts
in the mirror,
during a rainstorm.

the fluorescent yellow blares,
screeching commands that only clutter
the solemn wind with echoes.

there is nothing more
holy than honeycomb
or the spine pushing
through your skin.

this candle,
steady in the
flickering dark,
is a violent
form of love.

your eyes
closing shut
is the heartbeat
of the world.

I'm finding ways
to express my devotion.
I bought you a present
and wrapped it in a
little brown box.

I'm required to submit
a verdict: God
or no God? I choose
God, because
nothing could be more
vague than God.

my mother collects
little bowls and
places them
on the windowsill.
they overflow
with rainwater, and
we cup our hands.

in perfect history,
creation was practical,
a potter's wheel rhythm.
hands in the clay,
monotony made beautiful,
we spun ourselves
into vessels. but
our history is broken,
a linear landscape, as
endlessly fascinating
as splayed hair.

loss may be a form of passing
through, a hole we fall through.

winter fosters an intentional
architecture. my breath exits
like steam exiting an engine.

I've melted into a mirror,
a puddle of rain. this
window, the only crack
in my sky, is beloved.

the sour
voice of
the ocean
tells me
my first
communion
will taste
nothing like
the sun.

my dialog with God isn't going so well.
the universe can be domineering
in its bluntness, in its subtlety.

it's the forced domestication
of sadness that causes flowers
to wilt on the kitchen table.

the cement can only soak up
so much rain. the sidewalk
shimmers about to spill.

Spikenard

I miss spring and
the holiness of death
on the horizon.

the owl watches me
and doesn't turn her head.
it's nice to be loved
with such intensity.

battle is a proud thing,
it opens you. we flower
in vehement impasse.

my tea is full
of bitter tannins.
the night loses
its purple as
the mouth of
morning parts.

empty pots have been
slammed against the earth.
the sky is finally free.

the smallness in my heart
is big sometimes, its flowers
are more like fireworks.

the bathwater
is tepid. I recite
my biography
into the drain.

eggplants are oval,
each one a different
squashed circle.
there are too many
perfect things,
so, I will venerate
the illogical curves
of a frumpy purple
vegetable. I will blend
its egglike inside
into baba ghanoush.

Through the Rain

it was hot in the car as we drove through the rain.
water ran down the windows, blurring everything
except the already hazy glow that poured out from
the street lamps. the broken droplets caught the light,
transforming it into a watercolor painting. vague
but certain, this perfect representation defied
the Heisenberg Principle. physics ceases to function
after a couple of hours on the road. nose pressed
against the cold glass, you forget there is cement
beneath you. the present is obscured by its
continuous consumption. my mother had her hands on
the steering wheel, her eyes elsewhere. I reached
for the radio dial but thought better of it. we hadn't
stepped on the brakes yet. that was music
enough. we were flying with dream-like dissonance,
our bodies separate from our movement.

American Poetry

I imagine my brand-new copy of The Best American Poetry 2021 lying stiff and silent after the apocalypse. I'd like to remain conservative a little longer. save seed for winter. watch it sprout in the spring. I break bread by myself, sitting on the floor, hunched over by the fire, like God's lap cat, watching it snow. I'm hoping another ice age will give us room to thaw again. our Christmas tree this year was thirteen feet tall. I was just grateful that I couldn't reach the top. sometimes I want God to step out from the center of the sun. but other times I want Him to stay there, pinned, the tallest branch stuffed up His ass. this winter, I've noticed how the sky grows blue every young night, how it's growing, inching that much closer to everything. I'm thinking about how close blue is to orange. I'm thinking about how the snow hasn't stopped falling, about how I want to make a perfume out of all our empty orange peels, about how the mountains will melt into mud. on the unfinished walls of the century-old hardware store my grandparents turned into a home are portraits of the salmon they caught. more than alive, the fish tread water in their frames; open mouths, a gateway to heaven. glorious iconography. a paint brush, a pen, a knife. as I walk through the storm, I look back and see the windows tinted red with light. holy. the flags are flying, flopping like dying fish as they learn how to breathe. who is going to cut a hole in the horizon and let out the smoke?

Quilting

she made a quilt because
it was something to make
> out of scraps of cloth, out
> of stitches so tiny they
could be dark matter, or
the DNA God is ashamed
> of having. she has stories,
> singularities that shift with
the geometry of dawn
when morning has been
> forgotten. that's why she
> uses too much pink, but
strips the pale red polish
from her fingernails. she
> is tapping a counter rhythm
> on the countertop, like
a sewing machine, like
a machine singing its soul.
> she is trying to find the flesh
> she surrendered at the door
to His house. I want you
to set the church aside.
> I want your quilt to tell
> me how you never drove
off any cliffs. I want to hear
how you traced the shape
> of every edge you came
> across, how you stitched
without sealing: a beginning
and a middle and an end,
> how you sewed something
> to keep you warm, to keep
you breathing when your own
name becomes the ledge.

Apart

a wall away, I hear my mother scraping pots.
I'll never know what's beneath her skin. starlight,
fifty-two-years-old, good wine slowly poured.

it's a silent evening, metal on metal, bone on bone on
blue sky. day under night under night under day.
raw and wilted, the sun replays, light on light on

light. in a distant room, she is still scraping.
there's gunk underneath my fingernails, between
flesh and a hard place. I can almost, almost,

pull myself apart.

3 AM in the City
Allen Ginsberg
and the Body

outside my window there is a boy who shoots
blanks like bullets. in bed, I count my spine's
vertebrae. I'm learning to use an abacus, learning
the language of prayer beads. I've begun to hate

how I howl, calling everything holy. I've begun
to love the boy who hates. I open the window,
stare down the barrel of the gun, the face of God,
and see only my reflection in the floodplains

of concrete. I start counting until numbers sound
like sentences, like puddles of dead raindrops.
I begin to fold, folding the flesh so one shot tears
many holes. the boy pulls the trigger. he doesn't

aim at my window. instead, he shoots the sky
and continues preaching: hell is real, hell is real,
he says hell three times. hell is holy. you are all
going to burn. but he can't see that I'm already

burning beautifully.

Revolution

it is in my nature to throw

pebbles into the perfect

obituary of stagnant pond

water. revolution can be

a divisive philosophy of

being, a melody of firsts,

of thirsts. I am full of water,

circular rivers, water that

knows it has a place in

my heart, in my lungs, on

my tongue, spilling like

a river that has already

found its way to the sea.

Spring

1

on our tippy toes,

> we dance to a tambourine.
> it's a terrible thing to feel yourself tingle

on the crest of a wave that's going to crash.

> new-grass sorrow,
> full of green smell, dying,
> hot sand, it rained yesterday.

> caught in a storm drain,
> cherry blossoms are struggling
> under a dry breeze.

> awake, wrapped in our jean jackets,
> we swelter and freeze.

2

Mama, our umbilical cord was never cut.

> Mama, this is why
> I lace my fingers through yours.
> Mama, this is why
> I hide under my sweaty sheets.

Mama, the sun carries scissors.
Mama, Mama, Mama, I never should have left your belly.

3
what if, instead of being the bile that rises
in our chests as we spin around and around
the merry-a-go-round, time was the circle itself?
around and around we'd go, growing and dying
in the wombs of our mothers, watching the moon
change phase. we wouldn't shiver come spring,
fresh and fearing Ragnarök. in the ancient
creation story, Father Sky God seeds Mother
Moist Earth. lightning strikes. it's a myth with
a beginning, and presumably, an end. but what if
there were no fathers? a blasphemous thought:
the mother, the daughter, and the holy spirit.
Russian nesting dolls filled with moist earth.

4
the sun rises.

icy March, boiling April.
        thick socks and stinky feet.
we've already started to die.

alas, we drum our beginnings
        and dance to the tingling beat
of an implied ending.

Mama, I should never have left your belly.

Green

take a seat at the piano, moored
in a moorland, motherland. it's like kissing
or gardening. learn how her lips part.
we all open differently. we all thirst
differently. remember the sea.
you are never far from the sea.
everything is a sea. everything is a desert.
that's why we spread our fingers,
keep pounding the keys until
melody is informed by melody, rhythm by
rhythm, until there is no distance
between melody and rhythm,
until the melody of your breath
helps you find the rhythm of your body.
keep hitting the same chords
until a song rises. imagine hands sowing
grass across the earth. seed by
seed, until green is something rabid.

RED

God is real because/ Red is thick enough to paint with/ because we can use our tongues to trace the face of a demon/ when it's dark, when we're bored, when we need fire/ Red, not the red of a stop sign or the American flag/ but Red, a Red that's gone sour and sweet and bitter/ like a pomegranate seed stuck in its shell/ or the Red, the almost Red, the almost more than Red/ of her lips/ Red is proof that God is real/ that God drinks the same wine/ that God laughs at dinner parties and cries after the guests have left/ that God lusts and lives and loves/ but there's another Red/ a Red that's more than God or the Devil or a Sunburned Face/ a Red found in the scream behind stop/ in the threads of a flag/ in the heart of a pomegranate seed/ in her throat/ in the grapes that grow from the earth/ a Red too beautiful for us to love

Hunger

hungry for a sun I cannot eat,
I create my very own vernacular.

remember, there is no distance
between you and your metaphors.

sometimes, I want to burn the
garden God planted in my belly.

Free

it's supposed
to snow tonight.
I feel the ground
freezing.
I'm finished.
I'm free.
I'm ready
to break into
the breast
of the world and
learn how
it breathes.
tell me, tea kettle,
shall we sing
with one voice,
one violin,
one violence.

I Don't Know How to Pray

I don't know how to pray. Last year, out of curiosity, I hauled myself to the top
of the hill at seven in the morning to attend mass at Saint Mary's Star of the Sea.
I wanted to experience Catholicism: the ritual of eating God on a dreary Sunday
morning. But the service was conducted in Spanish. I didn't understand a word.
I live near the ocean.
Asleep with the windows open,
salt seeps into my dreams and my wounds.
They say downtown, resting peacefully at the bottom of the hill,
could be underwater in the next fifty years.
But still, I can't seem to earnestly ask the almighty atmosphere for help.
I'll mouth the occasional sarcastic request.
Or if I am feeling particularly melodramatic,
I'll kneel at the foot of my bed and beg,
just so I can use a big word like prostrate in my next poem.
They say religion is the opiate of the masses.
But I am fed up with living soberly.
It might be nice to overdose.
Then, at least, I'd be destined for heaven.

Bed Sheets

my room is:
the center of the sun
space whittled open
a lampshade
smooth sandpaper
where flowers die
colored glass
stomach-lining
a seed husk, a hull
a mouth without teeth.
a domesticated rainstorm.
candle wax melting
space between my palms
God's shed skin
crayons still in their box
a closed book
winter's taxidermy.
formaldehyde on my fingers
the sweaty side of the window.
music without speakers
rootless thunder
compost breathing

(Metaphorically)

I never went to church.

                yet I write about God

(metaphorically)

                I don't know why I still
capitalize the G.

a tourist crying in a cathedral,
I feel like an imposter.

there is such honesty in faith.
I am a liar.

Samhain

the child dons a sheet, cuts
holes for her eyes,
and the costume becomes
a prayer shawl.
just for this night, she wants
to be holy, haunting
the town, the forgotten
graveyard, God's rigid
exoskeleton. I'm a vessel,
she whispers, for this evening
of wind and ghosts.
rub lemon and sugar
on our teeth and watch
as bone becomes something
light can shine through.
I'm my eyes and nothing else.
I see. I see what separates
me from the storm brewing,
just past the warm yellow
glow of the neighborhood's
windows. I wish for a mantle.
I wish to be a lampshade.
I wish to flicker tonight, God's
breath blowing in
instead of out. this star-sown
veil of dark, simultaneously
raised and lowered, vanishes
the road-wide distance
between me and my soul.

Winter

on this highway,
the car hasn't stopped
colliding, consuming,
continuing.
the delicate flock-like
dance of a
million moments
is distilled into
a single impression
that shifts with
the passage of time
and glows with
the curves and vestiges
of its previous shapes.
each year we drive
to my grandma's house
for Christmas,
through a pastel valley

                where we meet
the swans

          on their way south.

Topless

I'm topless, sprawled
in the winter sun,
drinking plain mint tea.

                              my pale breasts rise
                                 from my chest,
                         a landscape of solid ghosts,

puncturing the boney
earth of my breath,
like a mountain or a mole.

                               I've found a place
                              where life is stripped
                         of everything but its glare.

the light illuminates
reality with such ferocity
that the world hides

                              behind its reflection.
                              I close my eyes and
                                imagine a spring.

Perfect Forms

my friend found the shell of a dragonfly

lying by the side of the road.

squeezing its torso, she lifted it into her hand.

I flinched.

how could she so casually touch a Dead Thing,

pluck it from itself and

place it in the realm of perfect forms,

the realm of palm-held offerings?

Plato, fuck your republic of the dead!

our world is not a world of shadows,

but of bone, sinew, and glue.

my friend is a true artist,

a curator, a scientist, a grave robber.

she carries formaldehyde wherever she goes.

Between

is it strange that Mary Oliver reminds me of Hafiz,
especially in the irresponsible dawn hours when I feel
like I could swallow God even before I swallow
my dreams, when the ghosts of swallows still dance
in the light of a swallowed sunset, when there is
nothing but blue inside, between these white pages?

The West

here, the graves
are worn away
by the rain. here,
the city is clean.
it tingles. glass
skyscrapers
and demolished
cathedrals are
ghosts, carrying
bells and mirrors
that only ring
in summer.
here, you let
an epitaph hover
between your
throat and lips
because the only
sacred thing
is what you still
haven't said.

From the Shell

from the egg, a spring flower
grows. its roots are suspended
in yellow yolk. it opens to the
blue sky. there is a flower inside
the shell as well. it doesn't know
blue or yellow, or the color it
will become. a question unfolds:
is the sun a mother or lover?

Rosemary

they put rosemary in hot water,
and we burn our lips, talking
quickly between sips. our singed
tongues stealing whatever they
can from this pine-pricked night
in late November. we are thinking
what we dare not ask: where did
they get the rosemary, where did
they find needles with enough
summer to be more than a drug?

The Heart

sometimes,
I hold rust and
call it red, because
I know there is a heart
beating, beyond the blue sky.

Panentheism

1 window

To make a paper snowflake is to experiment with symmetry, to hang it in the window is to experiment with worship. The same statement can be applied to stained glass, religion, or reality. Recently, I came to the translucent conclusion that God is light. Many philosophers and theologians before me have come to the same conclusion. It's a metaphor that is quite consistent with a theological label I encountered several weeks ago: panentheism: the inherently paradoxical idea that God is both inseparable from the universe and transcends it. Light is also paradoxical. Enmeshed in its reflection. And just like light, God exists as both a particle and wave.

2 towers

When I was just beginning to become conscious, paper snowflakes were one of my favorite crafts. I loved to see my cuts simultaneously transposed and recreated. As I brushed the scraps from the table, I began to realize that there was more than one layer of reality under my fingernails. It was like dropping a pebble in a pond, composing a poem, letting the rain wash away my footprints; it was one of my first experiences with God.

My cuts were echoed, my creations, my notions of creation, were exquisitely precarious as negative space was multiplied, then filled by the infinity behind it. After a while, paper snowflakes began to feel too fragile, as did algebra, as did skin. So, I returned to the garden, to a more corporeal form of magic. I built fairy houses and brewed tinctures and talked to trees. The fairies moved into the houses, the tinctures cured my headaches, the trees talked back. God was the dirt not the sun: less pernicious, less independent, less cruelly incomprehensible, less bright, more real... less real.

3 thoughts

In a fit of teenage rebellion, I've become attracted to a more conventional monotheistic God. And while I could never have the faith of a Bible-bashing Christian, I'm infatuated with the aesthetics, the horror and glory of organized religion. I long to feel the ruth and the ruthlessness of a sunburn, of a palpitating heart.

The ferocious divinity of Spanish poet Federico Garcia Lorca, who I have been obsessively reading, hasn't helped this perverted desire. I long to echo his passionate, holy declaration: "I am an anarchist, Communist, libertarian, Catholic, traditionalist and monarchist."

Like any good grown-up, not any good poet, I've been trying to find a responsible between. I've gone back to hanging paper snowflakes in the window. I've theorized about a symbiotic relationship with God, turned myself into a microbe that gives life to the big lumbering shell of the universe. But despite the limitations of our eyes, light is so much more than the paper it shines through, than the colors it is reflected in. Light is darkness, true-black pigment, full of everything imaginable.

Jump

I went down to the water just before it got dark.

I sat on the seawall with my knees close to my chest and smelled the salt. The water was gray, but it reflected the burnished purple of the sky.

How many times have I skinned my knees on those rocks? How many times have I broken myself open and got sand in my wounds? I feel rugged and ripe. I suppose that is what comes from living in a beautiful town situated on a crumbling cliffside.

I bruised the seagrass until it smelled alive.

The Earth and the Sun

"The mysterious power which everyone senses but no philosopher explains."
—Federico Garcia Lorca

I fall asleep reading about duende, reading, radiating duende. That's what Lorca's poetry does: it causes my grandmother's pitched voice to tremble with a terrible softness, like the moon liquified and stored in a jar. God, I've used the word duende, the second most sacred name, so many times lately. I've used it to explain everything that can't be explained. I hope I haven't cheapened it with desire.

For a moment, I trick myself into believing that the Spanish street names are more than an echo, that the baked brown hills of Santa Barbara are the Andalusian mountains Lorca rhapsodies over. As I trot down to the dust-strangled creek, I feel a piercing, euphoric scream rising in my chest: *Seville to wound! Cordoba to die in!*

The cliff we're perched upon could crumble at any moment, flinging us towards a sun that grows bigger each day. Duende, duende, duende! But what happens when there is nothing left for the sun to burn, nothing left except sun? I've thought a lot about death, but not annihilation. The distinction between the two states is a fundamental one. It's a distinction that has fueled artistic ecstasy for millennia. There is tension in death. And that tension remains until the last flower is blackened. But annihilation is monotonous. It's God's last weapon, last pure providence. It's a fire in which not even the demon Duende can survive.

A Place of Worship (Manifesto)

The cathedral was big, absurdly big. It towered over the cobblestone streets of Chartres's medieval center, imposing its harsh Gothic symmetry on a place that otherwise seemed to exist in a state of perpetual pastel charm. I stared at it, biting into a baguette. The cathedral was impressive. But being a twelve-year-old atheist, I had chosen to stop at the bakery before starting my sightseeing, even if it meant sacrificing the opportunity to experience mass. I found the baguette and the gentle June sun a far more sacred form of communion. I finished my bread, then entered the cathedral. I was curious to see a building with such a fascinating and ancient history, but I was ambivalent to the faith that drove the miracle of its construction.

The air was cooler inside the cathedral. It smelled like old stone. What struck me first was the singing: tremulous notes that seemed as old as the walls off which they echoed. Despite my bakery detour, mass had found me. I looked up. The arches rose to pointed pinnacles with a solid grace. The cathedral was composed of curves accented and grounded with the geometry of angles. It was dark, yet in that darkness lived so much color. With an almost ascetic sensibility, precious sunlight filtered through windows stained with stories, touching the gaudy marble of the partially refurbished walls.

Juxtaposition brought out my reluctant spirituality. The cathedral was a place of contradictions. There I first saw a detailed depiction of the crucifixion: the grotesque, yet passionate image of self-sacrifice was bathed in the soft glow of candlelight. I stared at it, horrified, while a glorious aria played. The grace of this place astounded me. A small melancholy ache rose in my chest, like I was missing or maybe longing for something. I could feel the careful geometry with which the architects had sought to please God. I could feel the many hands that had dedicated their lives to the cathedral's construction in poignant faith. I realized that I didn't have to be Catholic for this place to be holy. Its story made it sacred.

In that cathedral I found pieces of myself that didn't fit, yet I felt whole. For a moment, I let myself become part of an established and complex rhythm. I let myself dance with history. This experience was incompatible with my atheism. And in the years since, I have become an agnostic. I believe patterns are sacred: the ones we follow, the ones we seek to understand, and the ones we create. *Notre Dame de Chartres* was full of patterns of religion, architecture, and art.

———

These patterns created a throbbing amalgam of humanity and math, of logic and faith. As a writer and aspiring linguist, it is my dearest ambition to translate this amalgam into something I can understand. One of the defining characteristics of humankind is our ability to create stories, our ability to believe in things we cannot necessarily see. Sometimes the things we are not able to fully understand can be the most beautiful. And the process with which we attempt to make sense of these mysteries can be even more exquisite than the enigmas themselves.

After leaving the cathedral, we returned to the bakery to buy another baguette. We took turns tearing off chunks of the long loaf as we meandered through Chartres. But while we walked and ate, my mind lingered in the cathedral. Despite the early summer flowers, I could still smell the musty stone.

The Kitchen

We spent the first half of the day in the kitchen, slicing zucchini. The food was vegan, of course, so there was a lot of zucchinis to slice. I can't remember exactly how we ended up at the conference. Maybe we followed an ad on the school bulletin board, maybe somebody gave us tickets and forgot to mention that we'd have to work for them, maybe it was something our parents had encouraged us to take part in. Regardless, my friend and I stumbled up to the volunteer coordinator at the Global Earth Repair Summit, lost, giggling, and ready to make a difference.

I'd grown up surrounded by radical ideology. The people around me were viscerally attracted to the notion of revolution, of wiping the slate clean, of digging their feet back into the earth, of forgetting, of remembering. My neighbors were an odd mix of conspiracy theorists, communists, pot-smokers, and puritans; retired hippies who were torn between the peaceful retirement they felt they were entitled to and the stage they didn't want to give up yet. Needless to say, rhetoric was burned like incense.

I was a self-declared socialist who had just got back from a trip to Copenhagen. I was reading Sapiens, organizing school walkouts, and absolutely convinced I could build a better society from the ground up. When you're fifteen it begins to dawn on you that civilization is just one big problem, but you still haven't lost faith in a solution. Like you did when you were a child, you view adulthood as an unclaimed utopia. Before young intellectuals find something to hold sacred, even before they start reading the existentialists and decide nothing is sacred, they are convinced that the world should grow up with them.

It took four hours to chop up all the zucchini. The pieces had to be exactly two inches thick. My friend cut her finger and donned a clumsy rubber-glove. I found several rotten squashes at the bottom of the box. We listened to the man working next to us as he recounted his adventures. He was a former biology student in his early twenties who had dropped out of university to do his own eco-friendly version of van life, biking across the country with a tent and a guitar on his back. He chopped zucchini really fast and soon moved on to onions. I remember feeling jealous of how he maneuvered the knife with such prediction and grace. I wanted to be at home in my body, at home in the moment, like he was.

After the four hours were up, I was feeling exhilarated; a little bit exploited perhaps, but very bohemian. My wrists were aching, and my lungs were burning from the smoky kitchen. I was part of the movement. Clutching our volunteer passes, my friend and I went to examine the calendar of events that were being held that day. Angrier than we knew, we decided to attend a lecture on ecoterrorism.

The lecture began with a story about a radical group in Nigeria who were rebelling against extinction by waging a war against the oil industry. The group would set off bombs to halt the destruction the oil-mining was wreaking on the environment. "It comes down to direct action. Direct action is our only option," the man presenting asserted. He then warned us that most likely we wouldn't survive the coming tide change. That without the amenities of modern life, the amenities consuming our world, we would be lost. But he called on us to make the ultimate sacrifice. He called on us to annihilate civilization in hope that we'd give future generations the opportunity to build a better one.

The speaker was a wack-job, a martyr, a die-hard revolutionary currently under FBI surveillance. I left the room feeling like a Jacobin, a Bolshevik, a member of the New Left. But the flames in my stomach quickly soured. As we waited for my mom to pick us up in her fossil fuel burning car and take us out for tacos, I whispered to my friend: "maybe he's right, maybe violent action is the only way forward." She nodded, then changed the subject.

The terrifying part is that I'm still not sure. I've gone through the stages of adolescence. I've read the existentialists, I've discarded the existentialists, I've found things to hold sacred. When I reflect on that conference, I learned the most from the time I spent in the kitchen carefully, lovingly, slicing zucchini; from finding community in the drudgery of making ratatouille; from doing my small bit to prepare a sustainable meal. But I'm still not sure. I'm still not sure if we should blow up our oilwells, our libraries... our kitchens.

Rosewind

Brambles can become an extraordinary number of things, if you are willing to brave the thorns. They can become a cathedral, the light filtering through the tangle of wild roses like stained glass. They can become a home if you are sad enough, a ship if it's windy enough, a universe if you are small enough.

The first boy to venture into the Rosewind Cohousing Community rose bushes was playing capture the flag and desperate. He flung himself into their spiky arms to avoid getting caught, to protect the flag he'd claimed. He tunneled through the brambles until he had reached the clearing around the old hawthorn tree at the center. This was his capital. But, in time, after he'd gone to college or high school or middle school or wherever boys go when they turn tall, it became our capital. This was where we held our secret meetings. This was where we stored the junk food we weren't supposed to eat. This was where the adults couldn't fit. This arching gothic cavern was ours alone.

I would soon turn tall as well. But I could never imagine being taller than Avery, and he still managed to squeeze through the tunnel. When Avery stopped coming to council, I began to get nervous. Our country felt fragile, like jello melting under the relentless August sun. We needed validation, fresh faith. Were our borders too secure? Should we be inviting people in, instead of keeping them out? We moved our Kremlin to the playground.

This new location had its perks. It was obviously modeled after a castle. It was more accessible to those with poor imaginations and thin skin. It was closer to the community gardens where we could pilfer strawberries for our store houses and watch them rot on the hot splintery wood. There were monkey bars to walk on top of, swings to climb, and a short green plastic slide to eject our enemies from. The aching planks still creaked and shook in the wind. I was content for a while. Even though our circus shows attracted less crowds than we'd hoped. Even though our strawberries turned to sour jam. Even though, on the open sunny lawn, there were no monsters or thorns laying siege; we could still battle each other.

Childhood is playing capture the flag. It's running though rose bushes because you know there's a secret reason it's worth the scrapes, the blood, the twigs in your hair. It's fighting for something that changes every moment, for your country, for your body, for the future imprisoned in the brambles, in your dreams.

Saeta

My mother tells me that when I was little, I would lie in bed, exploring my phonemes.

I have been reading Lorca lately. I hardly speak a word of Spanish, but my chest swells with each syllable I whisper.

"La Lola / canta saetas" saeta, sa-ee-ta, sa-eta...

Saeta (pronounced sah-ATE-ah) is a dart, an arrow, or a piercing song from the Andalusian region of Spain. In poetry, saeta can exist simultaneously as a dart and a song. Both its sound and shape pierce the heart.

I like it when translations leave the poetry raw, senseless and full of sense. Like a child I feel my way through, delineating my own precious shades of passion.

Even as a toddler, I was flabbergasted by the vastness of language. One of my clearest memories from those blank slate years was of wondering how my mother accomplished the herculean task of teaching me how to speak. Like all kids, I asked the inevitable question: where do babies come from? But what truly concerned me was a different question, or at least different layer of the same question: where does language come from?

There was such majesty to the notion that even sound had an edge, to how you could so easily fall off and end up in the senseless sea. But even as a young child, I understood that words were only trees in the forest. Language had a shape. I could feel it in my mouth, see it in how nouns seemed to be made up of lines rather than matter. It was immense and intricate and wonderful. It wasn't something I could trace, but that didn't stop me from trying. Contemplating language was like reaching out for the edges of the universe, or the edges of my consciousness.

I recently learned that petrichor, the cumbersome academic-sounding name for the smell of rain hitting the dusty earth, is derived from *petra*, the Latin word for rock, and *ichor*, the blood of the Gods. Blood from rock, now that's something truly divine. Language, sufficiently deconstructed, can almost always be reduced to poetry, to paradox.

See, the thing about language: it fossilizes. If you analyze a word closely enough it shows the process by which concepts become complicated, that is, the process by which they are explained, the process of growing up.

Building with Pebbles

Some time ago, when I was young but conscious, my parents showed me a picture of my first snow. I was wrapped in a green blanket and wearing a strawberry hat. My mom held me close to her chest, but my eyes were wide open.

The present is always influencing the past. I like to think that I remember what it was like to be that little baby. I like to think I know what it was to be alive. But the truth is I only have my own preconceptions, my own extrapolations, taken from that photograph. I have only the desire to be desireless, to live in a world full of fresh snow.

My first authentic memory is actually of filling myself with desires, of becoming human.

When I was two or three, I would sit on the porch, wedging pebbles into the cracks between planks. When the stones didn't fit, I bruised the wood. To fill every tiny gap was the very first goal I remember setting. I think the emptiness bothered me.

I would examine each dusty pebble before finding it a place. I would rub it between my oily fingers. I would hold it to my mouth. It smelled like determination.

Children, almost awake, have a certain gluttony. When we are young, we require things to make sense. And we are content defying logic to avoid uncertainty.

I never mended my porch of imperfection. But I can still feel the ache, the tangible thrill of an impossible project, of methodical faith.

Iconography

It was misty that morning. My eyes were slow to wake. But when they finally flickered open, they caught on a glimmer of gold, the shiny cover of a thick tome stashed on a bookshelf in a corner of my grandma's attic.

Closer examination revealed that it was a book of saints, a coffee table encyclopedia of Byzantine icons, a bible for the agnostic art historian. I realized, in a flash, sun pouring in through the window, that it was my eighteenth birthday, that it was time to choose my saints. Everything was about to solidify into something blue and bright.

The twenty eighth of August is my time to make sense of the numbers etched into the clock face, the symbols scrawled onto my soul, the words I repeat to myself in the bathtub. Eighteen years. Eighteen chances to pray for something new, to make myself anew.

The Airport

My feet are untied, not my shoes.

At the airport, the windows are broken. Fresh air-conditioning pours in. It's a place caught between, a place where something meets nothing, yet everyone has direction, self-possession.

This is surprising considering the indecency of it, lots of glass, naked walls, the bare bone sound of a suitcase dragged across a marble floor, security guards badged and booted, passengers in pajamas. There's a vulnerability that comes from being alive, from leaving your life behind.

My mom told me that until recently she didn't realize "languishing" had a negative connotation. And why should it? Our fast-paced society is built on necessary restbites, the run before the jump. In this modern world, full of betweens, we yawn, sweatpants sagging, heels clicking, as we wait to fly. But we can fly, and isn't that amazing?

As we are already stretched thin: sprinting, sleeping, stargazing, perhaps it would be better if we let ourselves become translucent.

I peoplewatched in the airport today. I let myself stare. I untied my shoes. I let the people walking forward, eyes on their destination, walk through me.

And we were beautiful, all of us breathing air.

Down the Road

When I first ate a rose petal, I was seven and wanted to be a flower fairy. It tasted bitter like summer sunlight—summer, sunlight, bitter, a flower floating on the ocean of my tongue. I haven't described the experience till now, but that's what it was: a collection of associations burned into the shape of a moment. I had begun to compose poetry. Ever since putting that petal in my mouth, I've been a curator—not a collector, a curator. I could care less about stones, stuffed animals, and stamps. But I treasure the feeling of cracking open a geode or watching my black cat as her yellow eyes flicker awake, or licking a letter shut.

I've always maintained that perception, in and of itself, is an artform. It's an artform I aspire to practice with care and discernment. Moments can be composed like photographs, minutes like songs. For me, walking down the road is an act, not an experience. I weave a tapestry from spring grass and dewy spiderwebs because I'm afraid I'll need something to keep me warm when winter comes again. I live in one of the most beautiful places in the world, yet I don't fully experience it because I'm determined to live in my world, in the moments I've curated. I've started to treat my life like it's a museum, touching everything, but afraid to let anything touch me, lest it should disrupt my preconceived notion of the whole.

Today, as I walked to the park, I trotted down the street with the intention of seeing rather than perceiving, but it was like trying to meditate, frustrating and counterproductive (I even ended up composing parts of this essay in my head). When I got to Chetzemoka Park I surrendered my efforts, cracking open the poetry book I had brought with me, So What by Taha Muhammad Ali. After about forty pages, I emerged out of an arid Palestinian landscape: his gravelly, honey-sweet voice, the bare-bones and ripe-melancholy of his heart, and into the lush Pacific Northwest spring. I left my carefully chosen spot in the dappled shade of a magnolia tree and ran down to the water, to the exposed expanse of ocean. I truly saw the blue, rough and wild and utterly indescribable in its individuality and its wholeness.

It's strange how reading the Palestinian desert, the stark beauty of Taha Muhammad Ali's thoughts, helped me to truly see my exterior surroundings. Experiencing another's intimacies allowed me to escape my own. For a flash of a second, caught between two halves of the world, on an undefinable precipice, I was able to feel the earth's roundness. I think there are two kinds of searching—narrowing and opening—and they rely on each other. The linear concrete street I walk down is inherently a filter, a two-dimensional reality of hedgerows and magnolia trees, but it leads to the sea, where, still throbbing with poetry, I picked a whole rose, not just a petal, and let it slide, through my fingers, into the water below.

I'll take you to the orchard
and show you my God,
how we eat, juice dripping
from our open mouths.

I recently learned that the apple is
part of the rose family. I love how God
makes it so sweetness can swell, filling
the dry bones of language with flesh.

excess:
I'm chanting
what I could
easily write:
glory, glory.
glory, glory, glory.

it's new doctrine that
all statues must
become fountains.

the begonias
are burning.
I imagine
them burning
as my skin
turns pink
under the sun.

in the fish's stomach,
the sea writhes.
it has no room to dance,
yet still it thrashes,
pushed and pulled
by the moon.

on my knees in the raw heath,
I pray to my own smallness.
I need to confront the empty
plain of my hungry stomach.

I've been thinking about pride.
it feels like a cold pistol becoming hot,
like tears right before they stain your coat.

you speak of death
like a naked man
addresses the sky.
oh, to be roofless!
to stagger towards
the heat-heart-hearth
of a burning bible!

being the sun
is the next best
thing to being alive.

don't take a pickaxe
to the moon, or a broom
to the spiderwebs
in the corner, but light
a candle under the sky
and watch the moth
wings ignite. fire is
better when it is warm.

iconoclast could
become a form
of iconography as
thunder cuts another
hole in the sky.

a dot inside a star,
a star inside a dot.
alive, we fill our
wounds with salt.

my room still has its baby books,
with their pages of life-things permuted
into ordered sets: A is for apple.

in a ferocious cacophony of
fist banging, weed, and Neruda,
my grandparents dared to boom
the smallest possible questions,
to build good soil, to plant a garden.

metal to metal; sweating and
sea ready, he mends his boat.
we drive through the blue
shipyard, listening to Christmas
carols. we slow to watch his
ceaseless fire as it pours into
the gray water. little songs
become big in the singing.

sitting under the ineffable
intricacies of a hawthorn tree,
I am freed from simile. oh, sun!
you are what you shine through.

on the grass, beside
the playground,
a man rocks
to an unseen rhythm.
he has lost
himself, but found
his body and his God.

graph paper is not as solid as it seems.
the points where lines meet
are thrumming with new flowers.
our world is a binary one,
made of parallels and perpendiculars
and passionate collisions.

I think you are
God, because
all I remember
is your love.

Spikenard

last night, I
anointed the moon
with spikenard.
I called her Sophia.
we danced
a little before
I found my way
to the confessional.
she was shining
through the grate,
curiously watching
as I prayed.

the smell of wet grass
triggers the primal part of me
that fabricates tears.

there is a sourness to Eden,
a green apple sitting in the shade,
the geometry of almost touching God.

it was raining, and
the clock couldn't
match the rhythm.
our train was late.

the finite
and the infinite
are codependent.
never stop
swallowing
the sun.

last night we drove to
my grandma's through
the dusk and I started
crying. because the road
goes both ways and
home is directionless
when you are tired and
you know that you come
from many wombs.

I'm full of warmth
on a bone-wet day.

I've summoned a rainstorm,
but my body is a burning cathedral.
there will be tulips this spring.

Spikenard

I'm a Michelangelo
who hasn't read Plato.
I retrace your curves,
to make perfect
what was whole.

you brought morning.
my candle was snuffed
as needless in your arms.
we cannot see beyond,
but inside this room
everything is bright.

I want to read: "God is dead,"
to quote it with conviction.
after some Nietzsche,
smirking into the haze,
I will be a pious unbeliever.

I sit under a silver tree,
waiting for it to rain again.
the yellow leaves tremble
with the leftover weight
of last night's downpour.

my window is
not so much
a window as
a way to frame
the seasons.
the slanted light
seeping through
is the honey
of the moment.

sculpt a witness
from clay. give it
sad eyes. tell it
to frown when
you smile.
never forget
the smell of dirt,
or how you will
decompose before
your sculpture.

sometimes when the sun
sneaks into my eyes, it's
as round as a baseball or
the moon. and I wonder
if it could be contained in
a circle of orange crayon.

a desert feels
more like a dream,
like a drum, like a drum
with no resonance,
a dead drum, a drum
filled to the brim with life.

with a hum, I die slowly
like a violin. with a hum
that cannot die, I open,
a flower, or a symphony,
in the dark of its love.

how many years
do I have to live
with unnaturally
ripe strawberries
and swans that
have decided to
stay for winter?

like a fugitive, hiding in my skin,
I will probably still love you
when all my songs are sung,
and when I've forgotten we were
once something more than clay.

cycling along
the flat cement
at sunset, we
hear the frog
song. it swells,
candid and
all-consuming.

Orthodoxy

I was discussing Christianity with my mother. I am not a Christian. She is a liberal one. I was trying to weave a historical explanation for the differences between Catholicism and Eastern Orthodoxy, differences I had read about in a book by a presumptuous academic.

I was sitting in the park, bathed in the golden light of sunset and the smell of almost dead grass. I felt so whole. Too whole for half-guessed details and hesitant claims. I flopped down on my back, staring up at the unfathomable sky, and uttered a generalization just as vast. Religion is our way of making God tangible.

My mother paused; her forehead creased in thought. She told me she was not sure if she agreed. She shattered the hopeless perfection of it.

Open

1

the church was locked.
I rattled the handle, trying to force my way
through the smoked glass door.
it was noon and hot.
I just wanted God or Love or Shade
or perhaps to drink the Holy Water.
I cursed the Pope, slammed my fist
against the hard-orange, cherry-wood frame,
then turned back towards the street.
I stood in the middle of the road,
my fingers splayed, the sun pouring over my head,
in through my hands. slowly,
I walked back towards my house,
retracing the path I had etched down the hill.
this is what four years have come to:
a school in the distance,
an empty church on a hillside,
a road, a home. should I pray?
right here on the concrete, between steps?
or should I wait till next week?

2

here is the church
and here is the steeple,
here are the doors
and here are the people.

I feel only my bones, curved into trusses
under the weight of an absent faith.
my rib cage is a fist of hidden fingers,
reaching towards a heart of empty space,
pulsing dully, hungry for mass.

I cannot open:

the church
or the steeple
or the doors
or the people.

I hear the priest mumble, again and again,
what sounds like a prayer but is actually an offering:
body of Christ, body of Christ, body of Christ...

but these hands are pressed shut and unsatisfied,
unsure how to pray, how to capture
the silence between psalms, between their palms.

these bones are not stone
and this body is not bread.

3

a person
 is a church
   is a window

is the sun setting at the end
of the lane.

leave your shoes beside the door,
because here we are holy

and wrapped in sheets that
could be funeral shrouds

if we want.

or we could never die,
and instead, wash each day
in the morning rain.

a person
 is an altar
   is the glass
is the sun sheltered
behind the clouds.

Mint When It's Raining

someone once asked me what I like in my tea.
I said that if they could guess I'd believe
in God again. this being a Christian country,
they poured milk and honey into my cup.

I still haven't decided how I'll end up taking
my tea. sometimes I want starlight. sometimes
I want to taste my own bitter blood.
and sometimes, I just want God to promise

me paradise. Mama has made a game of it.
every time I cry good water, she brews me
a remedy. she sets the kettle boiling and starts
talking theology. mint when it's raining.

I've loved every drink she's given me,
from the milk in her breasts to the salt
in the sea we're swimming though. my poetry
is a confession written in a language

only God can understand, but she always tells
me exactly what I mean. she is both my translator,
my prophet, and the source of every waterfall.
she captures the weather of the world in a cup.

all I do I drink. poetry is three-souled.
it's hot steam and tea leaves. it's the sun
and the moon. it comes from a woman,
a woman who is both a woman and a womb.

New Day

I'm finding flesh under my skin:
        pink and unseen.

hands pressed together in prayer,
lips sealed shut, eyes closed,
fetal and kneeling.

tender and raw:
        to be human is to wait for morning,

to collect mason jars
and save them for a rainy day,
to watch them fill up with sky-water.

I found something in the cloudy sunrise,
in the fresh touch of a downpour,
cascading with my blood-river.

The Apple

the apple is God's fruit,
carefully created, sweet
and bitter with longing.

when you open an apple,
it's best to be precise.
use the tip of the knife,

press and puncture, extract
juice from flesh, slam
the edge into the board.

all your cuts should be
symmetrical. that is,
all your cuts should pull

the soul from the soul.
just keep slicing, just keep
remembering what it is

to be whole.

Black Velvet

someone take a knife to the sky, slash it open like
it's a piggy bank, and start counting change. I want
to catalog everything I've ever prayed for. stranded,
on the mountain top, after the flood, Noah had only
one grain of wheat left. he left the seed on the dirt,
on the deck of his new raft. then, imagining it was
God, he split the seed with a pickaxe. the Big Bang
wasn't so much a beginning as infinity realized. last
night, my roommate was folding clothes by the light
of her phone. I was listening to Bach and imagining
gardens growing wild, roses with their roots on fire.
there are so many different shades of mystery, more
layers than a Victorian woman's underwear. Bach
is perfectly succinct, yet his music never truly stops.
stoplights and highways, the city outside my window
is bare to its being, bare like piano keys, burned
down to the bone by the acid of their road-song. I'm
awake. night sky is a storage space for everything
that was lost in the flood, for all the rainstorms that
let loose too early. it's sagging, held up by a single
C-note. I keep throwing spears into an impenetrable,
impregnatable monotony, keep listening to the songs
they sing as they fly towards their graves, songs they
sing into the black velvet draped over their graves.

Two Dimensional/Ten Dimensional

As I sat in the park today, the sun slowly burning my face, innocuous pop music pouring in from the construction site across the street, the world ended. And I am sure it is still ending, somewhere, sometime.

Even under the blue sky, my vision is very narrow, limited by a stagnant stubborn variety of concentration. I was sprawled out on my gingham picnic blanket, squinting at my book, when the sky fell.

A gnat crash-landed on my toe, its corpse explicitly real, unnaturally still. My foot twitched. Irritated, I looked up from my book. At first, I thought it was just a speck of dirt, but a second glance revealed wings and legs and guts. I scraped its splattered insides off my skin, grimacing at the black sludge on my fingernail. It's amazing how fast we go from something to nothing. Point A to Point B, it's a two-dimensional, ten-dimensional transformation.

I dug my fingers into the fertile earth beneath me. I tuned into the music: the radio waves, the radiation, my burning ears, my burning nose. Terrified, I raised my book above my head, blocking the sun.

Respite

home is a place
that doesn't take up space
in my memories.
it smells like boiling water
and uncooked pasta.
it feels like skin.
moment by moment,
nothing and everything
in between.
it's only early spring
for a few spectacular weeks.
we're only alive
until the cherry blossoms
dissolve under the rain
or the patches of sunlight
on the warm wood floor
harden into scars
and the rain stops falling.
life is like standing
under a waterfall.
it's the first shock
you remember
and the end, the opening.
life is sucking in air.
home is the rhythm,
not the melody.
it's the sunrises I've forgotten
lying in bed.
I love my home,
but I only miss it when
I am tired of living.

Highways

It's a clear day. The sky is blue. The grass is green. And we are driving down the highway. The journey is marked by spastic bursts of conversation. I press my nose to the glass and point. There go the suburbs, the farmlands, the mountains. We are squished between moments, reckoning with a folded horizon.

A highway is a strip of land, paved over, with bold yellow stripes running down its center. It's a dead snake. It's everything it has crushed, everything it has pushed to its periphery. And it's nothing, a vacuum with the sole purpose of transporting our consciousness from one location to another. A highway is a portal forced to exist in conventional space. It's a portal stretched thin.

My cousin says she finds the dirty dive bars and mangy strip malls, the nameless thousand-mile purgatory outside the parapet, enticing. She says that everything looks more cohesive when viewed from another dimension. But I am repelled. This vantage point, this collage-like impression of time, of space, is pieced together from glances out the window. And in the rare moments of clarity, moments when the clock strikes twelve, the world is revealed with merciless explicitness. It's unnatural to see things for what they are: flimsy, made of flimsy angles.

Surrealism makes me profoundly uncomfortable. The components of a scene are exposed, the curtain is drawn. It's like experiencing space without time's wavelike lull. There is nothing holding the landscape together, just sporadic glances out the window.

Bathroom Floor

we are formless when we pray
on the bathroom floor, after our
second shower, after we have
noticed that our skin smells like
soap, that we haven't stopped
hating the body contained inside
cleanliness, or the hands that
filled the tub, that drained the
water, that cup the running river.

I Contain

it was Walt Whitman who wished, who wallowed,
in a single starry language, I contain multitudes.
It was Lorca who loved Whitman. it is I who love
Lorca. it was Lorca who loved, who showed how
multiverses collapse into a single point, a point
burning with the hellfire of heaven, how there
is blood under everything, blood between everything,
how the sea stumbles sickened by squares. it was
Lorca who drew altars in sidewalk cracks and
showed how a city of broken glass and stop lights
is a river, how everything is a river. I salute you, death.
I stand on my tippy toes and tremble, because,
fermenting in my gut, you become something beautiful.
there are no roots, only rivers. there are no rivers,
only roots. my body is a tree. this moment is a tree.
my blind friend said that there must be trees in this city.
the air feels fresh enough to fly away. I contain
paradoxes. I contain. I contain. I contain. I spill.

Prayer

Sophia,
make me big.
Sophia,
make me pretty.

I will anoint my body
with spikenard
and dance for you.

I will force Him
to proselytize
Himself,
while we sit still
and laugh.

When the Hermès Ad
on the Back of Vogue Magazine
Spoke to Sappho

it was from a Hermès ad,
on the back of Vogue magazine,
that I found meaning
in the curve of my hips.
beauty is a gesture™,
and I've taught my body to dance,
I've learned that the divine can
be imprisoned in a brushstroke,
in the inky uselessness
of a woman's extravagant limbs.
I bought the next issue,
wanting to learn the proper
way to apply lipstick.
but the statement was gone,
replaced by something dull and
magnetic, forms build™.
I'm no longer teetering on bones
made to bear fruit, but
an apple falling, a goddess
making love to the moon.

Capitol Hill Autonomous Zone

At the beginning of December, I found myself on Capitol Hill for a poetry reading. I had some time to spare, so I walked around the neighborhood's green space, Cal Anderson Park. If you were paying close attention to the news, you might recognize the name as the heart of the former Capitol Hill Autonomous Zone, a self-declared anarchist community in the middle of Seattle. Ground Zero of the Culture War. A Beautiful Experiment. A Necessary Disaster. America.

The park was a little rough around the edges: graffiti on the cement, empty soda cans and drug-needles underneath the picnic tables. There were only a couple of people, wrapped in their puff-jackets, trudging through the puddles. The rainbow crosswalk, the rainbow bridge leading over the scarred road, had a fresh coat of paint. The grass was dulled by winter.

My mom lived on Capitol Hill in the nineties, majoring in dance at Cornish College of the Arts. Sometimes, I picture her: an artist, a newly converted Christian always arguing with the Bible, breathless, sweaty, beautiful, dancing down the street, having the time of her life, trying to understand life. Sometimes, she will tell me stories about her time on Capitol Hill, about the nineties, about fitting four people into a one-bedroom apartment, about thrift-shopping, about piano concertos that verged on poetry, about how she hardly had time to pause between performances, about the skinheads lurking in alleyways, about the wheel-in coffee bars on the streets, about her extraordinary friends, too many of whom died of AIDS.

I don't know what I'm trying to write. I don't know if this is a prayer or journal entry. I don't know what I'm trying to find. But what I found was the memorial at the center of the park: a tower attached to a fountain. Its fake windows were boarded up with paintings depicting a city full of color. I started crying. I started to hate Reagan like I hated Trump.

I thought about how sometimes hate is easier when you lose too much to love. I thought about the girl I kissed. I thought about how I never want to kiss a boy. I thought about how this was only secondhand grief. I thought about how I had no right to be sitting in this muddy park crying when just blocks and months away the police had brutalized protesters. I thought about how lucky I was to have a mostly safe body. I thought about what it meant to redefine freedom. I thought about how I should stop romanticizing the nineties. I thought about how each time the New Year comes around it feels like we're spinning a prayer wheel. I thought about how I needed to do more than pray. I thought about how God should step up to the plate and write a new book.

The Womb

do you remember when that tickling in our stomachs had a name?
it was called God.
the flowers bloomed to God's rhythm, and we danced in our underwear.
our families burned weed and bras and incense and dollar bills.
they used history as kindling and smoked out the stars.
but we didn't need to misinterpret Rumi to converse with the Beloved,
we were formed inside of Her.
we were drum-circle children, raised in an undulating womb.

now, my friends Bible-bash with Nietzsche.
Jesus is the cigarette butt of their nihilistic jokes.
I am not a Christian, mais je suis chrétienne.
I venerate beeswax candles and Hildegard and fragrant oil.
I find the hungry-void counterproductive, so I take communion
and feed the God growing in my belly.

let's sit on the steps on our front porch and watch the rain.
let's watch the earth dance in Her underwear.
falling water is precious
now the clouds have become pregnant with tear-gas and idealism.

let the rain pour down! let us take shelter in our temples!

Apocalypse, Ἀποκάλυψις!

Spring

open window. smells of honey.
can't breathe. too beautiful.
the year dies.

from the somewhere.
spring wind. snatches. loose pages.
airs-out. sweaty armpits.

flowers bloom.
time skips. around a maypole.
ribbons crisscrossed. wound tight.

life. a fluttering thing.
voluminous. paper chrysanthemum.
under the rain.

it has begun. the dust.
daisies have opened. stopped opening.
rhythmless. no rain.

Summer

the landscape is
naked in the summer,
thirsty for the rain
that will dull
its burning contours,
for the snow
that will sooth the bare
throbbing spine
of its mountains.
the trees are the parched

green of a migraine.
perched on
the sandy cliffs,
they stare at the sound
like a woman stares
at her own breasts

Fall

I want to wear your skin
as a christening gown,
she told me one night,
while we set each other on fire,
while our petals, our leaves,
our thorns, and things
fell to the floor.
I thought the point of a baptism
was to make yourself clean.
no, it's to make yourself holy.
there's a difference.
we won't have any skin
after tonight. we'll never be able
to wash off the red.
last September, I started writing
my own apocalypse,
because my lover asked me
a pitched question:
what's the point of writing
while the world ripens and dies.
it's autumn again,
but the hills are still burning.
and even though it rained yesterday,
the maples turned yellow
in a brown haze.
we've stopped talking about it.
instead, we wait till it's dark
and love each other.

Imagining

I see Sappho
in every sculpture
without a face, in every
articulation of form.

I walked through
a cathedral today.
I ran through a gallery
and I didn't stop

to think about
anything more than
the shape of the
artist's desire,

to listen to the sound
the rain makes on
the glass roof and
remember it's raining.

Soaked and Screeching

sometimes it feels like everything is wet
and burning; like your shoes, your pack,
the floppy five-dollar magazine you
picked up on a whim are soggy and
screeching, like you're a fire truck lost
in the dark with only the sound of its
own sirens to guide it, like the road has
become a river and you've got tires
instead of tear-ducts. I'm sure you've
had those days, when you can't find
change for the bus, when the pharmacy
doesn't take your insurance, when your
keys get stuck in your apartment door,
when you're short-circuiting in the rain.
I know water is supposed to soothe
the seething, but my veins are a race-
track, but this is Seattle and the sound
of squelching is as consistent as a
combustion engine. oh city, there's not
enough pores in your concrete. I wish
I could soften your bricks into clay
again, curl up and let you caress me
again, watch the rain become rain again,
watch it water the ground again, watch
it hiss into steam again, watch it kiss me
holy again. I love the rain. I love you rain.
I'm so lucky, lucky enough to feel faith,
to breathe for a breath, to listen as the rain
lulls me to sleep. my heart is a drum.
I'm loved like a drum. we need to keep
pounding until the city is tender again,
until the mud is soft enough for footprints.
until the mud is soft enough to dance in,
until the mud is soft enough to dance in.

Something to Hold Flowers

I found a vase today
in a flea market downtown.
it was brown and heavy
and more perfect than nature.
it stood squat, like it was
made from clay scraped
from the bottoms of my boots,
sculpted in the salty surf,
battered until it became
something breakable.

Yellow

the man who leaves yellow
zucchinis on our front steps

grows the sun from the dirt.
love isn't bright enough to burn

your eyes. it's just yellow, soft
like beeswax and the sign

telling you to slow as you drive
down our neighborhood road.

Spring Salmon in the Skagit Valley

No Pacific Northwest family reunion is complete without salmon. The fish is placed at the center of the table, of the altar, slathered in dill and garlic. Gathered in a loose circle, artichokes, asparagus, arugula, crusty sourdough bread, mayonnaise, and lemon wedges, all bow to the King. It's essential to choose the right fish. It must be fat, fleshy, and fresh. The salmon's got to have a soul. It's got to have the Skagit River still singing through its supple bones.

In the early 1970s a couple of Beatniks moved to Edison, Washington, a tiny hamlet in the Skagit Valley, with their two small children. My grandparents transformed an abandoned hardware store into an art gallery and living space. They created a community, a gathering place for poets and pot-smokers. And while hippie communes of the era have a reputation of being quixotic, transient, and ultimately unhealthy, the Edison Eye was different because it was, and still is, deeply rooted in a sense of place. The living room smells like slough and woodsmoke. You can see the Cascades, Olympics, and San Juan Islands from the attic windows, silhouetted against every horizon. Guy Anderson's paintings cover the walls. The high ceilings echo with Theodore Roethke's poems recited like children's songs. Sitting on the counter are newly cut tulips. But most of all, this sense of place comes from my grandparents' commitment to food, to the garden, to the sea surrounding us.

My grandfather was a fisherman, a killer, a lover, a mystic, someone who could look a fish in its dead eyes and see the storm. He was a big man with a booming voice and a tender heart. Before he died, he told us that he wanted to feed the fish because the fish had fed him. I remember watching the waters part for his rusty hulk of a fishing boat as we dropped his ashes in the Puget Sound. The salmon at the center of the table is for him; it is him.

The old hardware store was silent when my grandfather died. We sat, in a loose circle, clutching mugs of tea and the books he used to read. Someone, at some point, prepared some kind of dinner. All I remember is a sense of displacement. I could smell the slough, the woodsmoke, the dusty handwoven tapestry draped over my grandfather's empty chair. If I listened closely, I could even hear the poetry. But I couldn't taste home.

Though slowly, as I kept returning to Edison to hug my grandmother, to finger the books, to eat salmon in the springtime, my grandfather began to reveal himself. He was woven into the meat of the place. His body was made of salt and dirt and books and salmon. And though his ashes were scattered, he was still whole. Every once in a while, I could see his hazel blue eyes shining through those of a fish, or through my own.

Skagit Valley in the springtime isn't complete without salmon. A good salmon costs money, but we're willing to pay our tithes. In our family, we worship at the dinner table. We take part in the cyclical sacrifice of a salmon's life. Like us, it swam all around the Sound before arriving home.

My Mama/My Maria

1

the kitchen is a place of
creation and deconstruction.

it's where my mother
cooks artichokes,
and where, together,
we pull them apart.

garlic steam and burnt fingertips,
we prepare our sacrifice.

my body is my God,
my home is my temple.

let's eat, let's worship
at the dinner table altar
and sing praises
to what we consume:

our food and our love.

consumption is cyclical,
so, we'll gloss each other's foreheads
with our greasy mouths.

2

I love artichokes and Pablo Neruda and the poems we read around the dinner
table. I love how we stripped each other down to our hearts to fill our bellies,
to be full again. I love how there is no distance in consumption. I love how you
grumble in the kitchen and break our grandmothers' pots. I love how the electric
stove is nothing holy, but it glows red anyway. I love how we hold hands around
the dinner table. I love how we, bold women dreaming of each other, eat thistle
flowers in the dark.

3

the room smells like artichokes.
they're violently simmering in a pressure cooker.
Mama, how many times have I told you I love you,
mumbling the words on my way out the door?
even love is a form of deconstruction, a repressed explosion.
we'll wait till the artichokes are tender.
where to start, Mama? in your womb, in my home, under the rain?
I know you believe in God. but I only believe in you:
in our womb and our home and our rain
and your belly and your kitchen and your yellow coat and your God.
because you told me that you would love me to infinity and beyond.
when the artichokes are ready, we'll carry them to the dinner table.
did you grab the candles? Mama, this passion is incandescent,
a flickering rhythm too vast to understand.
before infinity reached longer than your arms,
I would count your freckles and gray hairs.
you were big enough to tell stories, and I was big enough to count anything.
we'll dismember the artichokes and dedicate our glee to Neruda.
Mama, you make a grand ritual out of living, loving.
after pulling the petals from their throbbing heart,
we'll dip them in lemon and mayonnaise.
my Mama, my moon, my Maria, I love you.

Night Kayaking

it's enough to be
in this body,
to rock this boat.

I'm more loved
that anyone
has a right to be,

and at a loss,
because there's no
need to find God.

Notes

"Through the Rain": The Heisenberg Uncertainty Principle is the notion that the position and velocity of an object can't be precisely measured simultaneously, even theoretically.

"Spring": The "ancient creation story" outlined in the poem refers to the many Indo-European creation stories that follow this trope.

"Samhain": Samhain is a Celtic holiday celebrated during the autumn equinox that was a precursor to Halloween. It was supposedly the day when the veil between worlds was the thinnest.

"Perfect Forms": A fundamental theory in Plato's Republic is his theory of forms, in which the philosopher asserts that our world is just a shadow or echo of the true reality, a realm of perfect forms. The artist, who is seen as a mirror rather than an inventive force, corrupts the world by attempting to recreate reality, further removing it from its source.

"Between": Mary Oliver and Hafiz are two devotional poets who belong to different eras and spiritual traditions.

"Untitled (I'll Take You to the Orchard)": Spikenard was a popular perfume in the Roman Empire. In the New Testament, a woman, some people think a prostitute, sprinkles Jesus's feet with spikenard. The male disciples rebuke her for wasting such expensive perfume when it could have been sold to give money to the poor. But Jesus himself lauds the gesture's beauty.

Sophia means wisdom in Ancient Greek. It's also by which some Hellenistic thinkers called the Abrahamic God's feminine half.

"Two Dimensional/Ten Dimensional": The book I held over my head was Pilgrim at Tinker Creek by Annie Dillard.

"I Contain": The beginning of this poem is a reference to Lorca's "Ode to Walt Whitman."

"When the Hermès Ad on the Back of the Vogue Magazine": The apple is a reference to Sappho 90.

"Spring Salmon in the Skagit Valley": The first paragraph of this essay contains a series of references to the Pacific Northwest's geographical and artistic landscape.

"My Mama/My Maria": Maria is a character in Pablo Neruda's "Ode to an Artichoke." The poem has a very special place in my family; so do artichokes.

Acknowledgments

These poems and pieces of short prose were influenced by whatever I happened to be reading at the time I was writing them. So, I would like to give a general thanks to **Annie Dillard, Ocean Vuong, Pablo Neruda, Anne Carson, Teju Cole**... and many other incredible authors who I have had the privilege to be inspired by.

I must specifically acknowledge the work of **Federico Garcia Lorca**, whose words have set my soul on fire. I'm not entirely sure I should thank him for that fact, in a similar way to how I'm not sure if I should thank God for life.

Some of the poems and essays in this manuscript have appeared elsewhere, and I'm so thankful for the magazines and websites that have helped me get my work out into the world. Many of the works were posted on the youth writing websites **Write the World** and the **Young Writers Projects**. "American Poetry" was published under the title "Frozen America" by **Rattle**. "A Place of Worship" appeared in the **Blue Marble Review**. And "Something to Hold Flowers," was published on the **Young Poets Network** as a second prize winner of their August Challenge #3. "Driving through the Rain" was previously published on **Teen Ink**. "Yellow" was published on the **Young Poets Network**.

I owe huge amounts of gratitude to all my mentors past and present:

Arianne True and **Laura Da':** you gave this book form, helping me translate my thoughts and feelings first into words, then into something that could honestly be called poetry.

Patrick Jennings: Thank you for igniting my passion for writing and for keeping it burning.

Susan Reid: Not only did the **Young Writers Project** help me find a wonderful community of other young writers, but the website, and you in particular, also gave me a space where I could see myself as a poet.

Will Giles and **Spokes:** Youth Speaks breathed rhythm into my poetry. Thank you so much for introducing me to spoken word and for building a space for young poets to spit fire.

The whole Team at **SAL**, in particular **Alicia** and **Indira:** you somehow manage to make emails as exciting as ice cream.

All my brilliant poet friends: thank you for the dialectics and for your rejections of dialectics, for pushing the bounds of what poetry can be.

All my friends, poets, people, and people who think poetry is stupid: thank you for making my experience on this earth one that is worthy of poetry.

Lastly, my family: at its core, this book is about your love.

About the Author

Zinnia Hansen is Seattle's 2021/22 Youth Poet Laureate. Zinnia is a poet and essayist from the Pacific Northwest. She is a first-year student at the University of Washington, studying linguistics. Her work has been published in *Blue Marble Review*, *Young Poets Network*, and *Ice Lolly Review*. She was a finalist in the *New York Times* Personal Narrative Contest and part of the Hugo House Young Poet's Cohort.

This book is set in Lust Text

Book design by Cara Sutherland with assistance from
Indira Dahlstrom and Abi Pollokoff

Produced and published by Poetry NW Editions,
an educational press in the Written Arts Program
at Everett Community College